Praise for *THE PATRON SAINT OF MAK*

"In the movie *High Fidelity*, Chicago's Rob Gordon confesses, 'I felt like a fraud. I felt like one of those people who suddenly shave their heads and said they'd always been punks. I was sure I'd be discovered at any second.' Tim Stafford's *The Patron Saint of Making Curfew* is the opposite of that. Whether sweating his way through a Civil War battlefield while secretly dreaming of waterparks, or popping tabs on a tape cassette to prove the seriousness of his love mix, or humbly begging his fellow teenage friends for a ride home from a punk show so that he doesn't miss his decidedly non-punk-rock curfew, Stafford and his poetry prove to be the opposite of a fraud. Rather, together they create a sweet, sober, and hard-won lesson on staying authentic—then, and now. Blunt, hilarious, and heartfelt, Stafford's debut collection is a knock-out."
—CRISTIN O'KEEFE APTOWICZ, author of *Dr. Mutter's Marvels*

"The poetry of suburbs to city, from mainstream to punk, from child to adult, of choosing the roads and paths ahead of us, these are the subjects attempted by many writers, past and present. The art is to do it from one's own unique and twisted perspective, which somehow, perhaps magically, reveals partial and whole truths for both the outcasts and inner circles to contemplate and enjoy. In Tim's work ,this is successfully achieved."
—JOHN JUGHEAD PIERSON, original guitarist for Screeching
Weasel / host of *Jughead's Basement Podcast*

"Whether you come from far-off foreign suburbs with 'Lake' or 'Grove' in their names or from the inner city with neighborhoods prefaced only with "South" or "East" in theirs, you will find your-self anxious to enter and navigate your way through the poems in *The Patron Saint of Making Curfew*, because Tim Stafford's terse lines and even sharper line breaks hit you like a punch in the arm from a best friend: simultaneously violent and funny. For Tim Staf-ford, suburban Chicago was more than a place that Hemingway called home, it was a place where CD towers rose like skyscrap-ers to house the voracious appetite of the kingpin of all Columbia House Record Club scammers, his older brother. Yet Tim paints an ethereal and intangible picture of Chicago in these poems. At times, Stafford's poems exist somewhere between the realms of

Modernism and Impressionism, as Chicago is always just a bit out of focus in these poems. Intentional blurs remind us that to suburban kids, the city exists as Oz does to Dorothy—always out of arm's reach, shrouded by the haze of distance. But what's always in focus in these poems are the tangible images. The things we can embrace or punch in the face: stolen hood ornaments, mixtape cassettes with the tabs punched out, rocks in our pockets, or shit-talking dudes outside the Mr. Taco. There's a rawness and urgency in these poems that can be found in the verbs and in the white space that surrounds the verse. Many times in this collection you find yourself face-to-face with a poem that has everything in common with a dirty-faced and dirtier-mouthed suburban Chicago kid, a poem that on the surface doesn't give a shit what you think, but underneath, where the real magic of the poem lives, wants more than anything to be seen and heard. Tim invites you to join him down in the wood-paneled basement where these poems live and breathe 'as long as nobody/fucks with the washing machine.' I invite you to do the same."

—JOAQUÍN ZIHUATANEJO, World Poetry Slam champion
and author of *Arsonist*

"I, too, was a youth once trying to hold tight to being young even while hungering for something larger swinging on the other side of the fence, while not always feeling the click in me was the click in others. And while I was never a young punk growing up in the suburbs of Chicago, reading Tim Stafford's *Patron Saint* brought many smiles to my face, returning me to the sweetness of the open-heartedness of it all, of what the world can offer us, small as we may have been. As Tim says, 'The good stuff is good when someone gives it to you but it's better when you're the one holding the knife.' And this book was a reminder of both these goodnesses."

—ANIS MOJGANI, Oregon Poet Laureate
and World Poetry Slam champion

"'Poetry' and 'entertaining' rarely partner on the dance floor, but Tim Stafford has fox-trotted a miracle of sorts with this chapbook. Stafford's a straightedge kid who can't dance, but he can sure write poems that strut to the beat and get the reader's feet tapping. This collection riots with narrative and coming of age in a laugh- and music-filled tour of Chicago."

—PETER KAHN, author of *Little Kings* and coeditor of *The Golden Shovel Anthology: New Poems Honoring Gwendolyn Brooks*

THE PATRON SAINT OF MAKING CURFEW

Tim Stafford

Haymarket Books

Chicago, Illinois

Published in 2021 by
Haymarket Books
P.O. Box 180165
Chicago, IL 60618
773-583-7884

www.haymarketbooks.org
info@haymarketbooks.org

ISBN: 978-1-642597-59-2

Distributed to the trade in the US through Consortium Book Sales and Distribution (www.cbsd.com) and internationally through Ingram Publisher Services International (www.ingramcontent.com).

This book was published with the generous support of Lannan Foundation and Wallace Action Fund.

Special discounts are available for bulk purchases by organizations and institutions. Please call 773-583-7884 or email orders@haymarketbooks.org for more information.

Cover design by Jourdon Gullett.

Printed in Canada by union labor.

Library of Congress Cataloging-in-Publication data is available.

10 9 8 7 6 5 4 3 2 1

This book is dedicated to the memory of Tom Sullivan

Rail-3 Forever

Contents

The Patron Saint of Making Curfew

There is nothing punk about an 11:30 curfew.
There is nothing punk about making sure my
little ass is in the front door at 11:30,
before my dad leaves for work.

Danny Espinosa gave no shits about my curfew.
If he did, he hid them in the dark recesses of his Ford Escort.

By "them" I mean "his shits,"
as in "deep shit,"
which I remind Danny is what I will
be in if I'm not home by 11:30.

There should have been enough time to
get back to our suburbs.
The all-ages show ended at 10:30.
But it was a slow night,
and the promoter was in no rush
to push us out into the frozen tundra
of Chicago in January.

Danny lingered near the merch tables,
hobnobbing with the bands who'd just played
and must not have the time restrictions I did.

Danny's copilot, John, was talking to a couple of girls
with bleached hair, dyed blue, fading to green,
from far off suburbs with "Lake" or "Grove" in their names.
It didn't matter which, because John would not visit them
because his car was older and shittier than
Danny's, which is why Danny drove us to the city.

I did not complain.
I had no car, and Danny never
asked for gas money,
but it was 10:45 and I had to go.

Danny relented with 45 minutes to spare.
An impossible task
on 1/8th of a tank of gas.
Though not as shitty as John's car,
Danny's car was still shitty, which is why
Danny Espinosa did not take highways,
opting for the red light-ridden and train-tracked
side streets into the gradual mesh
of suburb to city.

Once safely ensconced in the backseat,
Danny popped in a 90-minute mixtape
and promised I'd be home
by the end of Side A.

Straight west from 2646 Fullerton
through a hipsterless Logan Square,
past the supermercado where I first saw a
lowrider bounce with hydraulics.
Past Kedzie,
past Kimball.
Not till we passed Central Park
did we realize all the traffic lights were green,
green like the money we did not have for gas,
green like the hair of the girls John would never visit.

To become a saint, the nominee must be beatified.
They must have proven miracles, and this was his first,
because he never took his foot off the gas,
and the lights stayed green

past Pulaski,
past Cicero,
past Austin,
all the way to Harlem,
where the first red light greeted us
but swiftly clicked on its left turn arrow.

We proceeded south
through Hemingway's hometown,
past the billiard hall where I learned what it meant
to get hustled and how not to let
it happen to me.

As we crossed the Burlington Northern tracks
in Berwyn, I noticed the other miracles:
The gas tank was now half full.
The cigarette Danny constantly puffed
never burned to its filter.

Danny's tires squealed as he pulled off
Harlem and onto the road that cut
through my town.

The final song on the mixtape came on,
so we only had maybe two minutes.

Past the quarry,
past the adult video store,
the tiny car barreled down my block.
During the final chorus,

I leapt from the backseat,
trampled through my front yard,
bounded up the front steps,
reaching the front door
just as my dad made his exit.

He stared at me,
looked back towards the
clock on the kitchen wall,
and said

11:28
a fucking miracle.

Now That the Statute of Limitations Is Up, Let's Talk About All the Times My Brother Scammed the Columbia House Record Club

My brother was a kingpin
who measured his fortune
in jewel cases.

Boxes showed up on the daily
addressed to every person,
pet, and imaginary friend in
our house, only with an
extra letter in our last name.

My brother scooped them up
before our mom came home,
whisked them to the back room
where he amassed his empire
8–10 CDs at a time.

CD towers were purchased to keep up
with demand like real estate developers
trying to keep up with a
booming population.

His room looked like the skyline
of an ever-expanding metropolis,
a subtle flex on any visitor.

He didn't have one album
by your favorite band.
He had every album by

every band you had
ever heard of.

The bills would arrive
with slightly altered names,
each more strongly
worded than the last.

They'd given us their 8 CDs for a penny.
Now they wanted blood to be
extracted one $20 CD at a time.

My brother,
calm and dismissive,
simply informed them
that no one by that name
lived here.

He called every bluff,
dodged every threat.
Soon the bills stopped
arriving altogether.

He was untouchable. He was
John Gotti in a Metallica shirt—

a band whose entire
discography he possessed.

Cadillac Hood Ornament

No big deal—
a pop and a twist,
a flick of the wrist

is what I told the girls
down my block when they asked
about the Cadillac hood ornament
that hung heavy from my neck
like Catholic guilt.

I take what I want, I said
not believing a word,
thankful that my trench coat covered
my knees, which quivered like freshly
struck church bells.

I'll see you around, I said,
as I strutted back to my house,
assuming my role as
the altar boy turned badass.

I reached my front door
fifteen minutes before my brother got home,
sprinted up the steps to our room,

removed the hood ornament,
placed the relic back into its cigar box
that reeked of cedar and bad decisions,
and slid it back under my brother's bed.

Stealing is a sin.
Borrowing is just borrowing.
No need to confess.

Like Oz

I grew up knowing Chicago like Oz—
a hazy silhouette on the horizon,
a mountain range of glass and steel
that I was neither encouraged nor discouraged to climb.

It simply existed as an elaborate backdrop
to my childhood.

The kids on my block knew the city
from class trips, shortcuts to baseball games,
and stories from family who used to live there.

We cobbled our stories together to create
a catch-as-catch-can history.

To some, it was a boat trip down the river
with a bag of popcorn.

To others, it was a broken promise,
a lost bet on a sure thing.

When I got older, I landed somewhere in between
the postcard images and newspaper headlines:

A fear based off of someone else's experiences,
a joy based on my own.

But who was I to claim this city?
I was an interloper
picking and choosing my experiences
and retreating back outside
the city limits.

We were raised knowing that America
is the land of opportunity,
that our ancestors made great sacrifices to come here.
We grew up in the shadows of factories,
knowing the smell of smokestacks,
inheriting the urge to break away,
because if there's one thing Midwest kids know,
it's how to escape.

Ode to the Berwyn Dance Queens

Diamond Girls cruise down 22nd St
in black Chevy Cavaliers with purple
ground effects and kicker boxes
in their trunks, blast Z-95, B-96,
or the freestyle mega-mixes they get at
the kiosk in North Riverside Park Mall
that sells bootleg cassettes and
bootleg concert shirts that are as
stiff as the queens' bangs that are
teased to the heavens and cemented in place with
handfuls of Vidal Sassoon mousse
and lacquered with a coat of
Aqua Net hairspray
stick out from their foreheads like
unicorn horns
maintain structural integrity
while they do the Running Man
or the Roger Rabbit on the dance floors
of the sketchiest juice bars
the kind where the old dudes who
work at Structure and drive
white Mustang 5.0s
creep on underage girls
but the Berwyn Dance Queens
don't care because it's not
like it'll be the first time
they bust their manicured
nails shattering dudes'
noses like a piñata's
for talking that shit
leave them bleeding
all over their Z-Cavariccis

while the queens head over to Mr. Taco

which isn't the best but they're
open late so
it's perfect
pagers still get blown up
by hopeful suitors who
have to wait until tomorrow
have to come correct
have to work on
their dance moves if they
want to keep up

Mixtape Love Poem #7

Punch out the tabs on the top
of the cassette, so I know it's real.

Personally, I Think The Clash
Would Be Cool With Our Bootlegging

Finding a punk record at the thrift
store was like uncovering a lost artifact.

Finding an early Clash album
was like finding the Ark of the Covenant.

How it found its way into a bin full
of Styx and Barry Manilow records did not matter.

It only mattered that Danny found it.
He had a working record player,

the kind with a cassette deck to
dub copies for all,

to be played in cars,
to be played in boomboxes,

to be played at the skate spots,
to have a riot of our own.

This Civil War Battlefield Is Not a Water Park

for Dad

This battlefield is not a waterpark.
It is not fun for the whole family.

The only things that ever flowed
here were blood
and sweat—
my sweat,
my brother's sweat,
that cascaded from under
our White Sox caps
like overfilled buckets.

My mom and sister stayed in the car
blasting the A/C and New Kids
on the Block cassettes,
and I hated them for it—

not enough to shoot them
because of conflicting
views of slavery, but enough
to dunk each of them
in a wave pool
in a water park
where we definitely are not at.

There is no joy,
no relief from Virginia weather
at one in the afternoon
in July.

We walk through "Bloody Lane,"
a great name for a country road
where thousands of soldiers
drowned under a wave of
artillery fire, but a poor
name for a water slide
which I am not on.

My dad is not a lifeguard.
My dad is not a tour guide.

He is a drifter.
He floats through this field
as if he is wearing a life jacket.

We are rocks in his pockets,
keeping him down.
We cut him free,

find our way back to the car,
whip the doors open to feel
that splash of air conditioning.
Drenched only in sweat

we find a use for those towels
after all.

Anthony Bourdain Takes Me

to a Punk Show in 1979

"This ain't no Mudd Club, or CBGB"
—Talking Heads

He walks with a junkie's confidence
down streets that are as dark
as overlapping shadows.

The popped collar of his leather jacket
is all that protects him from the freezing
wind that, though blowing from
seemingly all directions, does not
diminish his ability to light up
a fresh cigarette.

I don't know how many blocks
we've walked from his restaurant
in a not-cool part of Manhattan
to this wasteland on the Lower East Side,
but he has already explained
the current state of punk rock
in New York City—

which bands broke up, who moved,
who OD'd, who died.
He's listed dozens of names, both
popular and obscure, the A-sides
and the B-sides, and I struggle to keep
up, because he is obviously on
speed. And I'm relieved he took
a bump with the boys on his

kitchen crew, because I'm afraid

I wouldn't be able to turn him down
if he offered.

Down the block he dips,
mid-conversation, into the doorway
of a broken-down tenement
any paying tenant moved out of
years ago.

We climb at least as many floors
as blocks we walked to get here
until we reach an
open unit turned
after-hours spot.

There is no cover charge for Tony.
He tells me he brings in the artists,
punks, prostitutes, and dealers
to his restaurant on slow nights,

claims his Spaghetti Bolognese
helped the doorman deal with
being dope sick.

I do my best to avoid eye contact with
the kid, maybe twelve years old, with a
spiked dog collar, who is growling
at random patrons that must be used
to this act because they don't
give a shit.

I'm surprised but relieved when the kid
climbs behind the drum set and counts
off *1-2-3-4* to kick off the first song.

Tony finds me mid-song and yells
in my ear about how great this band is.
Then he asks if I can find my way back
without him, because he's gotta
find a guy about a thing.

I tell him *no problem.*
He thanks me,
hands me a bread roll
he'd hidden in his pocket (still warm
from the evening's service),
and he is off.

Straight-Edge Kid Goes to a Rave

And he dances poorly to what will later
be described to him as "Trance."

His feet can't catch the rhythm
that undulates and buries itself,
crescendo upon crescendo,
as if his feet were looking for a beat
that refused to drop.

Condensation covers the walls and floor,
an unholy mix of sweat and humidity
mopped up by the cuffs of jeans
the size of sewer caps.

A girl wearing a Care Bears ringer tee asks
Straight-Edge Kid if he wants some coke.
Straight-Edge Kid wonders
if she has any Sprite
then remembers where he is
and responds, *No thank you.*

He is not having a bad time
despite the heat and lack of earplugs.
This is not his scene, but he
admires the DIY ethos
in play to pull this off.

He wants to be a good sport.
He wants to prove he can hang,

until the police arrive
at the exact moment

his friends are peaking
on ecstasy.

Straight-Edge Kid is
babysitter, smuggler,
superhero, and
designated driver.

He guides his friends out a back
stairwell with the promise
of freedom and pancakes
at the Golden Nugget.

Despite the swishing sounds
emitting from their oversized pants,
they escape into the 4 a.m. air,
bass ringing in their ears
like tiny echoes whispering
freedom.

The Flower Man at the Fireside Bowl

Never paid a cover because he's a local,
and if anyone else said they were local
back then they were a liar.

Holding a fistful of artificial flowers—
the red kind (sometimes white),
whatever kind he could get,

—held out in front like a lantern
to part the sea of tourists he hoped
to become customers.

2 bucks for one, or 3 for five,
and if you tried to barter
you were an asshole.

I heard a guy bought up
every flower he had, even
the folded and smashed ones,
packed them into the pockets
of his winter coat,

gave him a hundred-dollar bill,
and told him to keep the change.

The guy did his best to create a bouquet
before proposing to his girlfriend
onstage while their favorite band
played their favorite song.

I bought one once to give to a girl who
never showed up to see my band.

I gave it to our drummer.

Ode to the Hippies Home for Spring Break

Our friends turned hippies
home from university

greet us with their
shoeboxes of punk CDs,

milk crates full of punk vinyl
—residue of their past lives.

We're eager recipients of
their castoffs.

A mutualistic relationship
forged out of necessity.

For them, cash for fuel to tour
with the Grateful Dead all summer.

For us, music the record store would
label as "rare" and double the price.

It was kid's music, they'd say.
We don't give a shit, we'd say,

feeding at the crates
like pigs at a trough

too engrossed in the hunt
to realize our friends were moving on,

and we too, were
castoffs.

For Each Dude Who Thought He Was the First
to Play "Wonderwall" at the Open Mic in 1996

There is a line outside the coffee shop
that stretches down the block,
around the corner,
past the other coffee shop
whose line is just as long
but stretches in the
opposite direction
past yet another coffee shop
with its own line extending
into the distance.

Each line is packed with dudes
tuning and re-tuning the
acoustic guitars they
bought with graduation money
along with picks
hemp necklaces,
but no lessons.

A parade of talentless
zombies with frosted tips
extends into infinity,
waiting to play
"Wonderwall" to
an exhausted audience
with thousand-yard stares
brought on by
the endless renditions
of "Wonderwall"
each somehow shittier

than the one
before it.

Meager applause
fills each performer
with misplaced encouragement.
They don't realize the audience
isn't clapping for them.
They're clapping because
it's over—
a temporary reprieve
from the caterwauling
of junior college dropouts
with phony British accents
and limited musical
ability.

Dude, there will be plenty
of opportunities
for your mediocrity
to be rewarded.

Today
is not that day.

Exit Wounds

Your family blew our
block like a junkie
overconfident in his
ability to kick.

Mom said your mom
walked out of work
like she was a newly
crowned queen eager
to escape the peasants.

Dad grounded me the
day you left to make
sure I didn't get your
new phone number.

He didn't believe
in burning bridges.
He believed in
salting the earth.

In revisionist histories,
where your family
did not exist,

most memories of you
left when I got permission
to leave the block—

when I learned
proximity isn't the only
criteria for friendship.

Mom said your mom
came back to work
looking to get her job back—

a position long filled
by a boss with a shorter
memory than mine.

Dad said your dad
was full of shit,
would always stay that way.

Sister said she saw you
twenty-five years later but she
knew it was you

on a highway exit ramp
asking for change for gas
for a car that did not exist—

homemade tattoos track marked
up both arms without care
for style or aesthetic.

She told me the exit number.
I pretended to write it down.

The Metro

Remember when the Cubs were shit and Daley had yet to sell the city's soul in exchange for parking meters and even if you couldn't find a parking space you could park at McDonald's for like 6 bucks that you could pay for with the collected pocket change of the 8 kids we crammed into a Ford Taurus station wagon with an Operation Ivy sticker on the back and all you needed to bring was 10 bucks because the Metro was doing punk shows for 5 bucks which left you with enough money to buy a 7-inch record and a bean burrito at the Taco Bell the Cubs just tore down which means there is nothing left for me in that neighborhood?

Ode to a DuPage Basement Show

There are cool parents in the suburbs
who prove it by allowing their kids
to throw shows in their wood-paneled
basements so long as nobody
fucks with the washing machine.

Parents who go over to their
neighbors houses in the afternoon,
chitchat about weather and golf
then ask them not to call the
cops about the noise.

Parents who sit in their comfy
chairs reading newspapers
and waving to the parade of
patrons made uneasy by the sight
of supportive parenting.

Parents who know nothing
of the scene but who remember
that being a kid can be as brutal
as the heaviest riffs fighting
through the floorboards.

Straight-Edge Kid Steals a Bottle of Wine
from a Poetry Reading Because Class War

He's not sure what to do with it
as he walks out of the reading and across
the campus to his car, half expecting
a contingent of graduate students
in their autumnal sweaters
to give chase, make their brown
wingtips go clickety-clack
on the sidewalk like
Morse code for
We are rich kids,
and we demand justice!

This is class war,
he chants in his head,
the bottle bulging
from under his jacket,
a flag captured in
the name of the proletariat.

He was not supposed to be here.
He was the dork who got invited
to the cool kids' party and was
dumb enough to show up.

The evening started with students
of the poet-turned-professor
reading poems preceded
by anecdotes and inside jokes
like questions to a test he
never studied for.

The award-winning poet-turned-professor
read award-winning poems
from his award-winning book.
His students reacted
with *oohs* and *ahs*
to every line break,
every stanza,
as if the most vocal would
receive extra credit.

After the reading,
he cut through the crowd to get his
book signed before swiping the
unguarded bottle of red wine, left
by a fawning fan, just
because he could.

At his car, he fumbles for the keys
like a horror movie victim escaping
a pursuer, except for one
major difference.

There is no pursuit.
There is no chase.

He left the room the same
way he entered: a nobody.

Anthony Bourdain's Record Collection Goes Up for Auction

But it's not the one you want.

That one got sold off piecemeal
around the Bowery, because
drug dealers don't dig vinyl.

That collection,
an almost complete stockpile
of early New York punk records,
would have drawn thousands
regardless of who owned them.

This collection is
a haphazard reclamation
of original and reissued classics
culled from the racks of record
stores around the world.

The original could have
been replicated easily
with TV host money,
but Tony liked to dig,

to carve through a crate
of vinyl like a butcher
through a pig for the night's dinner—

discarding the prog rock and
jam bands like so
much gristle.

The good stuff is good
when someone gives it
to you, but it's better when
you're the one holding
the knife.

For the Beards of Logan Square

I do not like your beard.
Your beard is dumb.

Your beard is not a beard at all.
It is a shame blanket,

a crusted heap of calcified stalactites
running away from that smirk on your face.

The same smirk you give me
when I tell you I live in the suburbs,
as if you weren't from the suburbs,

or Iowa.

As if your beard didn't mark the
starting line for gentrification.

As if your beard isn't the reason
landlords started jacking up the rent.

Your beard remembers how this neighborhood used to be,
does not realize it's the reason why it is not.

Your beard is oblivious.

Your beard craves street credibility.
It brags about the shootings in your alley.

Your beard is arrogant.
It is not bulletproof.

It does not work for peace.

It does not worry about crime rates till its bike is stolen.

Your beard knows all the best bars.
Your beard knows where to get the best tamales.
Your beard thinks itself a soothsayer.
Your beard tells half-truths.

Your beard is a crusted heap of calcified stalactites
running away from that smirk on your face.

Your beard is not a beard at all.
It is a shame blanket.

Your beard is dumb.

No,

I do not like your beard.

Straight-Edge Kid Turns 40

And, finally, nobody thinks it's
weird he doesn't drink.
They just assume he's been
through some shit.

Acknowledgments

"Anthony Bourdain Takes Me to a Punk Show in 1979" first appeared in *FreezeRay Poetry* Issue 20.

"Like Oz" was commissioned for the inaugural WOERDZ Festival in Luzern, Switzerland.

Gratitude

Many, many, thanks to the following:

My son, Michael.

My partner, Hiu To.

Fam: Mom, Dad, Shannon, Matt, Angie, Eliot, Micah, John Paul, Avery, and the Pedersen families.

The Press: Maya Marshall, Aricka Foreman, Nisha Bolsey, Julie Fain, and everyone at Haymarket Books.

The Homies/Poets: Luke Kahun, Ricardo Cozzolino, Sean and Ninna Dorgan, Chris and Flavie Rose, Collin Diederich, Nicole Carlson, Antonio Vergara, Brian Healy, Vince Murphy, Dan "Sully" Sullivan, Joel and Beth Chmara, Robbie Q. Telfer, Aly Bosetti, Molly Meacham, Shelley Glaizner, Jon and Colleen Arturi, J. W. Basilo, Pete Kahn, Cristin O'Keefe Aptowicz, Marc Smith, Sandra Yau, Steve Stoll, Justin Howard, Dave Snedden, Katie Rinaldi, J. Tulungan, Jeff Guerrero, Chelsie Jangord, Jourdon and Chantal Gullett, Daniel O'Connor and the First Gear International Players Club, Britteney Black Rose Kapri, Idris Goodwin, Billy Tuggle, José Olivarez, Tim "Toaster" Henderson, Raych Jackson, Anis Mojgani, Marty McConnell, Emily Rose Kahn-Sheahan, Nate Marshall, Craig Zomchek, Shappy Seasholtz, Derrick C. Brown and Write Bloody Books, and the staff and students at West 40 Regional Safe Schools Program.

The Euros: Ko Bylanzky, Björn and Hilds Högsdal, Hazel Brugger, Thomas Spitzer, André Schürmann, Tanja Ahlin, Mitja Sesko, Gabriel Vetter, Peter Dyreborg, André Hérrmann, Tilo Strauss, Stefan Schwarck, Tobi Kunze, Sebastian 23, Lars Ruppel, Dalibor Markovic, Ken Yamamoto, Temye Tesfu, Zurg and Yopo, Nicolette Krutz.

The Coolspeak Clique: Carlos Ojeda Jr., Ernesto Mejia, Joey Negron, Natasha Carrizosa, Joaquin Zihuatanejo, Zach Gowen, Lilyan Prado Carillo, Juan Cangas, Justin Colon, Lamarr Womble, Chris Collins, Terri Lomax, Nicholas Bell, Gil Castillo, and Angela Vivar Romero.

The Artist: Jourdon Gullett and his most righteous cover.

The Sunday Morning Curb Crew: Jeff Gilman, Nick Kwasigroch, Pete Wiese, Larry Dobson, Ryan Whitacre, and Bill Wiora.

Pajama Boyz: Ryan and Justin Metcalf, Jon Tutaj and Tutaj BJJ, Sean Burke, and Force BJJ.

Special Shout Out: to Dan Espinosa, John Scapillato, and all the bands we saw thanks to Danny's Ford Escort.

About the Author

Photo by Hiu To

Tim Stafford is a poet and public educator from Lyons, Illinois. He is the editor of *Learn Then Burn: A Modern Poetry Anthology for the Classroom*, the all-ages anthology series from Write Bloody Publishing. He is a former Chicago Poetry Slam champion and he performs regularly across the United States and Europe, including at the 2015 Woerdz Festival in Luzern, Switzerland, and the ABC Brecht Festival in Augsburg, Germany. This is his first collection.